Daphne Wright
Home Ornaments

With essays by Francis McKee and Simon Morrissey

theartworksprogramme

Shelf Life: A Pocket Encyclopaedia

Francis McKee

A

Accumulators *Aye you never, I mean it was a parish in they days, but you never got money off them. You had to put in work.*

Aye, and the parish. They would not give you money. Tell you to pawn it.

Oh aye, you wouldn't get the money. They used to go round the houses.

No kidding they used to come round, James's mother told me this. There was a man used to come out. She had a wireless, and in they days there were batteries with the wireless.

Accumulators.

And they used to tell them to pawn it. So they would give them money.

Aye it was a luxury having a radio.

If you had a radio you were living in luxury.

My gran – we called it a wireless – my gran had a wireless and you had no electricity so it was…

Mantles.

The gas mantles you know and you put a penny in it and you lit this and that kept, but the wireless couldn't go because there was no electricity. So it was what you call accumulators…

Accumulators.

And you had two, so you took one up to the shop in Cumberland Street and left it to get charged up, and you got the other back to put in, you know.

Architecture When archaeologists started looking at the Greek temple precincts, they could not make out at first what principles of planning governed the relationships between buildings. They seemed haphazard and unaligned. It was not until the archaeologists unravelled the myths, and how the stories of creation were thought to inhabit the landscape, that they realized what was done. The buildings were placed in a landscape vigorous with meaning, they were set down, not in relation to each other, but into this – and I hesitate, to savour the phrase – this charged void.   Paul Shepheard, *What Is Architecture?*, 1994

Art   Contrary to what one might have thought, it was not machines that came to replace painting or written music, but the general technicity of man, destined to supplement nature, which for Aristotle was the definition of art: art executes the way nature does, that is, proceeding in relation to an end, but it executes that which nature does not. It is a great curse, and paradox, that under the words 'technique,' 'technology,' (Greek techne), we first of all mean the underlying mechanics of something, the machinery or instrument, then secondly, some kind of monstrous autonomous power we are unable to grasp. Whereas technology is us, in the constant execution of our humanness, especially since the Neolithic. Since then we have transformed, supplemented, and indeed partly destroyed nature. Thus today there is a singular conjunction or art and technology – technology stripping art of its 'aestheticity' and sacredness, as well as its characteristic gratuitous and decorative beauty, on the one hand, and on the other, an appeal, either a call, a question, or a concern, on the part of art to technology: how to provide something of the orderliness of meaning, but a meaning open to the fact of its own absence (what in fact art has always provided). The result is a technology I like to define as the operation of means toward an end that is not given. This is basically the same thing Aristotle was saying: Nature is what operates means, in and of itself, toward an end given by nature itself. The flower grows to become a flower. What disqualifies this model for us, the flower and 'the rose that grows without reason', is that the reason for the rose is the rose, while we don't know what the reason for our technology is, because we don't have the rose, that is, a finality. It was long thought that on the whole technology was moving toward both science and happiness – happiness as health or comfort, for example, or as mastery and ownership of nature, as Descartes had it. But it is very striking how much technology has now stripped and bared itself as not having ends. So we are no longer at all sure that it will provide happiness, and it becomes impossible to detach from it some entity like 'science' as absolute knowledge. But this also means rethinking ourselves as ends, as Kant said, not as beings that relate to and through given ends, but as beings having to incessantly initiate, rediscover, or rather invent their finality. Interview with Jean-Luc Nancy in Michel Gaillot, *Multiple Meaning. Techno: An Artistic and Political Laboratory of the Present* , 1998

Aura The German writer, Walter Benjamin, famously cited the damage caused to the 'aura' of any work of art by the development of mechanical reproduction:

> The authenticity of a thing is the essence of all that is transmissible from its beginning, ranging from its substantive duration to its testimony to the history which it has experienced. Since the historical testimony rests on the authenticity, the former, too, is jeopardized by reproduction when substantive duration ceases to matter. And what is really jeopardized when the historical testimony is affected is the authority of the object. … One might generalize by saying: the technique of reproduction detaches the reproduced object from the domain of tradition. By making many reproductions it substitutes a plurality of copies for a unique existence. And in permitting the reproduction to meet the beholder or listener in his own particular situation, it reactivates the object reproduced. These two processes lead to a tremendous shattering of tradition which is the obverse of the contemporary crisis and renewal of mankind. Both

processes are intimately connected with the contemporary mass movements.

Glasgow, however, is a city that defined itself through mechanical reproduction. The birthplace of the steam engine and a key site in the emergence of the Industrial Revolution, the city thrived by producing objects valued only for their capacity to be copied exactly.

Oddly, though, the areas where workers were packed into cramped quarters gained a sense of 'aura'. The Gorbals, in particular, has been looked on with nostalgia and sentimentality – its hardship interpreted as authenticity and its past density of population taken to represent a sense of community. In reality, the area was the arrival point for wave after wave of immigration – each generation erasing and rewriting the history of the locale. The perpetually shifting focus of attention within the area has left it without a centre and the regular exodus of its populations has left it in an amnesiac state. It is the more stable remainder of the city around it that preserves its memory.

B

Bakeries *A lot of employers in the area – bakeries, two big bakeries down here – the Co-operative had big bakeries – bread bakeries and cake bakeries – massive plants you know, that served most of the West of Scotland for bread and things like that, you know – and high, big employment, because these sort of things, they were intensive a lot of these things, you know …*

Benjamin, Walter By close-ups of the things around us, by focusing on hidden details of familiar objects, by exploring commonplace milieus under the ingenious guidance of the camera, the film, on the one hand, extends our comprehension of the necessities which rule our lives; on the other hand it manages to assure us of

an immense field of action. Our taverns and our metropolitan streets, our offices and our furnished rooms, our railroad stations and our factories appeared to have us locked up hopelessly. Then came the film and burst this prison-world asunder by the dynamite of the tenth of a second, so that now, in the midst of its far-flung ruins and debris, we calmly and adventurously go travelling. With the close-up, space expands; with slow motion, movement is extended. The enlargement of a snapshot does not simply render more precise what in any case was visible though unclear: it reveals entirely new structural formations of the subject. Walter Benjamin, *Illuminations*, 1968

Bread *Aye there was a lot of it. And do you remember standing in the queue for Milander bread? I remember bread.*

It was a bakers. The older women, the grannies, they used to like this certain bread. It were Beatties bread. Sunblest came after that, didn't it? When I was small I used to eat Milander. You had to wait and you used to have stand in a big, big queue to get served by this man. He also used to sell currant buns, remember the currant buns?

Aye.

So you do the Milander loaf and the current bun.

It was just a plain bread but it tasted different you know, especially baked.

Then we had the Scranshaw.

I was going to say that there.

It was mis-shaped stuff from the bakery and they had this shop and you would wake every Saturday morning and you had to wait in the right queue for to get these cakes and whatever was there but we came because you got it much cheaper. Because we couldn't afford things, so we went along. My mother would say Sarah next door needs such and a thing, Mary downstair such and a thing so I was a wee one for orders.

Aye. In the prams.

Aye.

10

In the prams, and you also got pies Susan.

Aye.

Size of a tea plate a flat plate, that's too big and it was bits of stewed steak in it and mince and they sold it. Two, two pence coins, that what you got that pie for, tuppence. All of the people they used to stand there sometimes in the week they were there for seven in the morning coming…

Saturday morning was my morning for standing there.

That's right Susan and they come at seven and they would wait until ten when that van came, wains playing on the pavements. They got lovely cakes.

My mum, I used to work in Graydons that's down the other way and it was a biscuit factory and I was off on a Saturday, but my mother used to book the washes for me. I never got off with it on a Saturday. I was up at nine o'clock, I went down to the steamie, I was there for three or four hours. Aye and my mother used to send somebody's wee ones down with tea and with a sandwich. If I was lucky somebody would come down with tea and a sandwich…

C

Cactus   The plant as paradox. Its domestic popularity rests on the fact that it is easy to manage. A cactus survives months of neglect and is therefore the perfect house-plant for the homeowner who is overworked. At the same time, the plant – in all its hostile, prickly desolation – evokes the desert, nothingness and retreat from modern life. The austerity and self-sufficiency of cacti speak to us from another world.

Community[1]   *So the houses were built for exactly 10 years and were emptied in 10 years and then demolished, and the land was held, and that's the new Crown Street now – Queen Elizabeth Square – all that land round about there, and where we're standing, was all damp houses too …*

JULES VERNE

JOURNEY TO THE CENTRE OF
THE WORLD

CAPTAIN NIMO

I think it damaged the community – I think it did – I don't think they can do things like that without damaging communities – they build a lot of houses and a lot of the people, the indigenous people had left, a lot of, not strangers, but a lot of people coming from other areas come in, and I think that damaged communities …

Community[2] A community is not a project of fusion, or in some general way a productive or operative project – nor is it a *project* at all … A community is the presentation to its members of their mortal truth – which amounts to saying that there is no community of immortal beings: one can imagine either a society or a communion of immortal beings, but not a community. It is the presentation of the finitude and the irredeemable excess that make up finite being: its death, but also its birth, and only the community can present me my birth, and along with it the impossibility of my crossing over into my death. Jean-Luc Nancy, *The Inoperative Community*, 1982

Cookers *I was in M & Ms.*

My sister was in Twomax.

I was only 14/15 when I was in there, M & M's sweetie works that was up the Oatlands wasn't it Susie.

And then the steel bits you cleaned with …

The sliders you took it off once a month and took it round, if you had a good slider you took it and got it chromium plated.

Chromium plated.

Once a month, you know, and get it chromium plated. Then when they done away with them and you got the interiors in you had to get a Seauchi cooker mind, a Seauchi cooker.

S E A U C H I was the name of the cooker.

Aye. Oh, you were a toff if you had a Seauchi cooker.

My Ma and Dad had one, she painted it up.

It was green and cream sometimes, wasn't it.

THE SCOTSMAN Wednesday, 4 September 2002 **9**

Focus On The Property Boom

IS YOUR FUTURE IN SAFE HANDS?

The Scottish property market is booming as never before, but can it last, asks *Frank O'Donnell*

FINDING out the truth about Scotland's housing market can be somewhat problematic.

Our newspapers, television programmes, radio and the internet are saturated with stories on property, accompanied by statistics which, depending on the day, can appear to contradict each other neatly.

"Housing Boom May Be Over" screamed the *Daily Mail* on 14 June this year. Just 18 days later, the paper's headline was: "House Price Boom May Go On For 20 Years."

And it is not just the mass media who baffle us. Yesterday, the Halifax, the country's leading mortgage lender, reported that prices rose by just 0.2 per cent during August. This contrasted sharply with its major competitor, the Nationwide, who found a 2.5 per cent monthly jump and an annual increase of 22.7 per cent – the highest since 1989.

This problem is exacerbated in Scotland because many of the surveys and reports emanate from London and the south east, where trends may be moving at a different pace. In Scotland, too, a two-tier market is developing, with prices in Edinburgh bearing little resemblance to the rest of the country. According to a recent Halifax report, the Ayrshire towns of Ardrossan and Irvine saw a price drop of more than 5 per cent in the last decade. In the same period, prices in Edinburgh soared by 121 per cent.

A new report by property consultants FPD Savills accepts that coverage of the market has become "increasingly frenzied" and is replete with "mixed and confusing messages".

So just where are we? Are house prices overvalued or undervalued? And can the boom last?

Buying to rent, long-term renting, significant changes in the way we buy property and fluctuating interest rates and prices all make for an uncertain future.   Picture: Ian Rutherford

Solutions for the first-time buyer

SCOTLAND'S property boom has become a headache for many first-time buyers who are now struggling to gain a foothold on the housing ladder.

With the cost of buying their first property soaring month by month – particularly in hotspots in the central belt – young couples and single buyers are now turning to more imaginative solutions for their starter home.

One such option is a mobile home, which can sell for as little as £3,000 second hand. Compared with the cost of a £60,000 one-bedroom flat in Edinburgh's Gorgie/Dalry, this is tremendous value.

Liz Lynch, an office manager at Pentland Marine Park in Loanhead, near Edinburgh, has been inundated with requests.

"The Edinburgh property boom has had a knock-on effect here. Last week, we had 70 calls with around 20 prospective buyers coming forward," she said.

"Buying a mobile home is a good way of getting into the property market and, if you maintain them, they can last an indefinite time. It can give you good collateral to move to the next stage on the property ladder."

Ms Lynch added: "I have lived here for over 13 years. It is a lovely environment; private, and has a good community spirit. I can't see past mobile-home life."

Another popular solution for prospective homebuyers

That's right aye.

Green and cream.

You never needed that when you had the range. Once you got the range in you couldn't cook on.

You couldn't cook so you had to get the Seauchi cooker and it wasn't as good as the range. Not at all.

The only thing was the cleaning of the range wasn't it? A lot of cleaning.

See I remember when I was young my mother got the box crib, two boxes either side and they were padded and you could actually sit in these boxes. It was that big crib thing this range and you could actually sit on these boxes and they could hold magazines inside, but see if you sat in this box and the fire was on there was great heat, really comfortable.

Crisps *Do you remember John Johnson that was a pawn shop? John Johnson on Marcus Street just near the picture house.*

Know where you are, aye.

The drapers. I used to go up there for my tights and underwear but the pawn shop there as well and in the back -

Aye but you got more money in the pawn in Cumberland Street.

You are right Susie, and we used to come down three stairs didn't you, is it one stair or three…?

Three stairs.

Crisp factory in the back of the pawn shop where they made crisps …

And the bakers…

Lots of people in the bakers on a Sunday night. Apply pie, won't it Susan?

Oh aye, lovely apple pie so it was.

D

Debt *John's mother had the 16 of them and she had a load of debt men came and they were put in the hat each week and that's the truth.*

For a raffle who gets paid.

Who gets paid and doesn't.

Yeah one night the old man, well my father in law he was doon the pub and John was with him and this one was at the door getting cheeky so he came in and he started on John's mother and she says to him if you don't get out the door, your hat won't even go in the hat (Laughs). It's true.

We can laugh about it now but that is the truth that.

You have got to take the hard times to enjoy the good.

Oh aye.

Dinner *And you had to do as you were told. I had a good man. Don't get he was great but he had his wee points. My first daughter was only a baby and I used to say to him, 'what do you fancy for your dinner?' So he wanted boiled cabbage and ribs but the butcher shut on a Tuesday and I was round my mothers because we always stayed round a bit and I couldn't get the ribs, so I got his a pork chop but at this other butchers. I made a nice meal, so I did. Amy was only months old, playing about and I will never forget this, it all cost money. I said, 'Is there something wrong with that?' He said 'No'. I said, 'Why aren't you eating it?' 'Because it's not what I asked for'. So I explained it to him. I says, 'I forgot Tuesday shutting'. Mind the shops used to shut on a Tuesday. Everything shut at one o'clock.*

'Well you should have got it before they shut'. I says, 'Is that right?' So I just lifted it and I scraped it into the bucket. He said, 'What are you doing?' I said, 'You'll eat the next I make', and I put it in the bucket. My mother always said start as you mean to end. And I mean I wasn't going to take that.

I bet he didn't do it again.

It was a perfectly good meal and he did like the meal, but because it wasn't what he asked for… Stuff him. Aye, and he was a good one. One of the good guys, by the way.

Dixon's Blazes *Dixon Blazes – aye, I remember it, aye I remember it, they used to tap the furnaces at night, the streets were all sort of … with the grid pattern, if you look at the old Gorbals maps, there's old maps in the Art room of the Old Gorbals – the old grid pattern, so if you look from the river right up to the top, and at night when they tapped the ovens, I don't know what they did, the whole place glowed red, you know, they poured the iron – oh, the whole place was like Dante's Inferno … aye, it just lit the whole place up …*

E

Edition In an art world where scarcity is the rule, editions unsettle and disturb the equilibrium of things. Value can no longer be measured simply by the uniqueness of the work of art and Benjamin's 'aura' makes less sense when the principle of reproduction is established. And yet, much of the power of the edition also lies in its limited nature. Time, and the inevitability of accidents and loss, will restore the natural balance.

Evolution It is interesting to contemplate an entangled bank, clothed with many plants of many kinds, with birds singing on the bushes, with various insects flitting about, and with worms crawling through the damp earth, and to reflect that these elaborately constructed forms, so different from each other, and dependent on each other in so complex a manner, have all been produced by laws acting around us. These laws, taken in the largest sense, being Growth with Reproduction; Inheritance which is almost implied by reproduction; Variability from the indirect and direct action of the external conditions of life, and from use and disuse; a Ratio of

Increase so high as to lead to a Struggle for Life, and as a consequence to Natural Selection, entailing Divergence of Character and the Extinction of less-improved forms. Thus, from the war of nature, from famine and death, the most exalted object which we are capable of conceiving, namely, the production of the higher animals, directly follows. There is grandeur in this view of life, with its several powers, having been originally breathed into a few forms or into one; and that, whilst this planet has gone cycling on according to the fixed law of gravity, from so simple a beginning endless forms most beautiful and most wonderful have been, and are being, evolved. Charles Darwin, *Origin of Species*, First Edition, 1859

F

Family photos Sociologists and theorists of photography have written a great deal about the role of the family album as a means of establishing hierarchy and societal norms in the domestic situation. But, no-one has discussed the family photo in relation to happiness.

Photos are carefully edited and only particular selections survive and enter the family album. Almost without fail, these are moments of happiness. Weddings, birthdays, holidays and nights out make the edit. Funerals are rarely even recorded and do not feature in albums. The scarce moments where happiness may possibly occur are saved. They are not simply evidence, they still have a power to uplift their owners.

Fidelma *(Irish)* A princess named Fiedhelm was one of Saint Patrick's first converts to Christianity.

Fish *The fish market was in there.*
We had a fish market as well.
Fish market was down the lane. I can remember that.

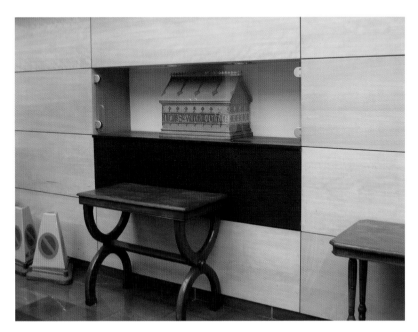

Remember the kipper store I worked inside the kipper store and people could come and buy kippers but there as well you saw the men go in with their Wellingtons and you could smell the kippers getting smoked. They used to put them under the smoke machine or something.

Floors *When I worked in Graydons, big bales of corrugated paper came in because the biscuits get packed into tins so the corrugated paper had to go in to stop them going soft. The bales were that height and it was kind of corrugated paper. It was round and I used to say to them when it was Thursday, 'Mind you keep me two of them.' And then it was the old tram cars. I would go on the old tram cars with these two wraps and I would go home on a Friday night. I would do the windows, do the stairs, wash up and these corrugated papers would do as carpets and the house was lovely. We used it as carpets.*

Just inside your door as well, weren't they?

Yeah.

I always put newspaper under my door mat.

Oh aye, aye.

I have always done it. I have not done it with the new because the landing was new lino down but I always put papers under since the old days.

I had the big, thick corrugated paper.

G

Gifts *The church, you never got anything from the church.*

No. My mother, never.

The only thing we ever got, when my mother died we got taken away for a day to a Christmas pantomime and it was the grey lady actually, Susan, and she came up and took us some children's books but they were already off of someone else. They were used because they had their names on them…

Oh it was terrible.

We put out Over 200 fresh items a day

24

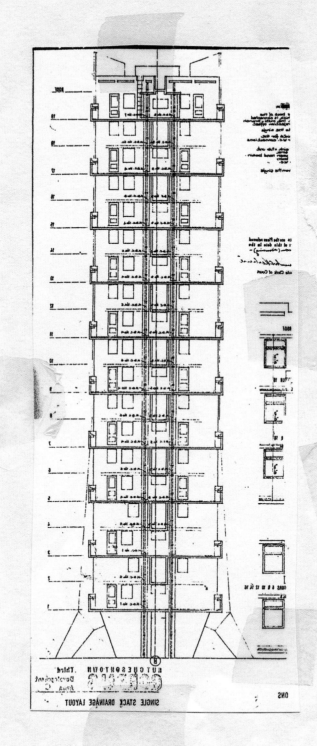

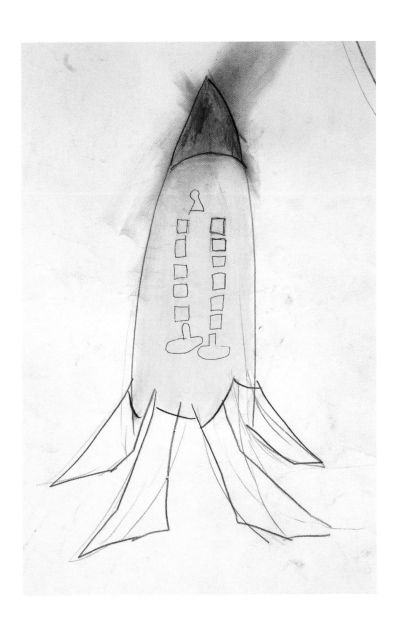

Gorbals *The first changes were the old tenements, eh, pre-war tenements, and after the wars the big drive to get rid of the so called 'slums' in the Gorbals, or so called 'slums' in Glasgow, and they decided they would call it a regeneration area, so they started demolishing all the old houses, moving the people to the new schemes in Castlemilk and Easterhouse, Drumchapel, and then, as they demolished parts of it, they started building again, as they built, they moved people from the old tenements into the new houses, but eh, some parts were a bit of a disaster, in the 60's especially, they built these sort houses, system built houses, concrete slabs all put together like Lego and apparently they were very successful in Marseilles, in the South of France – naturally they would be, they had the climate there for it … so when they built them here, there was lots of problems, dampness … I moved into one of these new houses from an old tenement, but and then the dampness, and that's how I started getting involved in politics and activity, because it started a big dampness campaign to re-house the people out of these new houses.*

Guinea Pigs Often known as 'sea pigs' by sailors who considered them an easily transportable form of fresh meat, their relationship with humans has been mixed at best. Regularly kept as pets, they are also synonymous with scientific testing (though they have been mostly replaced by rats and mice in that process). Their main value to medical research lies in the fact that they are one of the few animals that, like humans, cannot synthesize Vitamin C but must obtain it from diet. One scientist who used them for experimentation, Lord Lister, defended the act saying "There are people who do not object to eating a mutton chop – people who do not even object to shooting a pheasant with the considerable chance that it may be only wounded and may have to die after lingering in pain, unable to obtain its proper nutriment – and yet consider it something monstrous to introduce under the skin of a guinea-pig a little inoculation of some microbe to ascertain its action. These seem to me to be most inconsistent views. With regard to all matters with which we are concerned in this world, everything depends upon the motive."

Increasingly that scientific defence fails to convince critics and it is under sustained attack. The guinea pig, more than ever, is a controversial animal.

H

Housework *Housework and that, we had to do it when we were young. My mother died and there was six of us, she was 37, the youngest was three month and one was three. Alice was six, no Alice was seven, James was three, Alice was seven and I was nine coming up for ten, and my mother lived with us as well and we had to fend for ourselves, and my dad was working, Susan.*
I was oldest and my mother, and dad went away with somebody else and we were five and I was the oldest and my mother ended up with drink problems so it was left to me for, aye. So we have been through mills, we have been through…

I

Industrial landscape[1]

This town, is coming like a ghost town
Why must the youth fight against themselves?
Government leaving the youth on the shelf
This place, is coming like a ghost town
No job to be found in this country
Can't go on no more
The people getting angry

The Specials, *Ghost Town*

Industrial landscape[2] Towards the end of the twentieth century, a new aesthetic appeared based on the ruins of the industrial landscape. It was shaped in several great cities as they experienced the decline and disappearance of the heavy industries that had defined their prosperity. Manchester, Sheffield and Glasgow are the most obvious of these cities. These blighted cities quickly spawned dark urban horrors – the Moors murders in Manchester, Bible John in Glasgow. At the same time, the grim mechanical rhythms of industry were internalised by their inhabitants. Sheffield and Manchester became the birthplace of melancholic machine-like music – Joy Division, Cabaret Voltaire – while Glasgow became a second home to the founders of techno and house, exiled from other ruined cities like Detroit and Chicago.

J

Japanese Shinto altar shelf The Shinto altar shelf is seen as an exotic custom where ancestors and old relatives are remembered and honoured – an example of a culture which cares more for the past than our own in the west. But that yearning to honour the past exists for us as well and is visible in the very fabric of culture where the past is endlessly plundered and recycled. The retro nature of the media may be seen as a form of nostalgia or fashion but the process harbours something deeper as everything from melodies, to colour combinations to formal styles are tested repeatedly and the best are compacted, sampled and revived in new contexts.

K

Kitsch[1] Kitsch is mechanical and operates by formulas. Kitsch is vicarious experience and faked sensations. Kitsch changes according to style, but remains always the same. Kitsch is the epitome of all that is spurious in the life of our times.

Clement Greenberg, *Avant-Garde and Kitsch*, 1939

Kitsch[2] Kitsch is the absolute denial of shit, in both the literal and figurative senses of the word; kitsch excludes everything from its purview which is essentially unacceptable in human existence. Milan Kundera, *The Unbearable Lightness of Being*, 1984

L

Leprosy

Willie: The old father, he got treated there – where the Mosque is now, it used to be Hospital Street…

Bill: Gorbals Cross, it used to be Gorbals Cross …

Willie: Correct, because it wis a Leper –

Bill: For the Crusades aye:

Willie: Aye, they came back from the Crusades…

Bill: Catching all kinds of nasty things!

Willie: The Crusaders brought it back – the Crusaders brought it back …

Bill: Ah mean, a lot of them didnae hiv Leprosy, it wis diseases from houses of ill repute (laughing) – they were treated there, aye, Robert the Bruce's father, that's how you seen his face in the picture – he wis treated there …

Willie: He died the same death as King Solomon.

Bill: Gonorrhoea was it?

Willie: And King Solomon's thigh bones fell apart …

Bill: a full house, a full house –

Willie: He died o' a full house (laughing)

Long-Lived Birds Some of the longer living birds include the large cockatoos and large macaws. Zoos have documented cockatoos that have lived into their eighties. A Moluccan cockatoo at the San Diego Zoo was at least eighty years old when he died. Since he had been caught in the wild, his exact age was unknown.

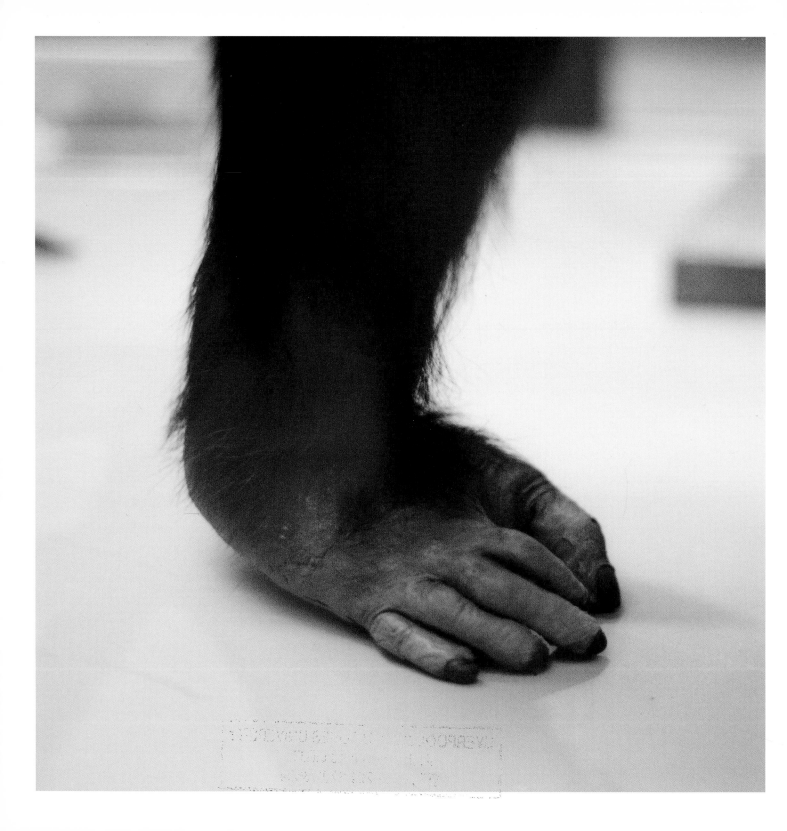

A Leadbeater's cockatoo at Chicago's Brookfield Zoo is the only animal left from their original collection – he's now in his sixties. Macaws have a prospective lifespan of seventy-five years, and the Amazons live to their forties and fifties. With the longevity of parrots comes the responsibility of providing for your companion beyond your own death. If you have a long-lived species of parrot as a companion, consider ensuring that the bird makes friends among your acquaintances, and that it is clear to your friends and family where your bird should go when you can no longer care for him.

Though the cockatoos, macaws and Amazons can be long-lived, they may also succumb at earlier-than-expected ages to many ailments. These include ailments linked to obesity and stress as well as household accidents. Larry Lachman, Diane Grindol and Frank Kocher, *Birds off the Perch*, 2003

Love *Even mothers and fathers didn't give you affection in they days. They didn't openly. No.*

Even man and wife in the house didn't openly give affection.

And you didn't get praise for anything you done good at school. Praise was never given to you.

M

Miscellaneous The Gorbals is Glasgow's hybrid laboratory, a constant series of experiments and unexpected cross-fertilisations that has produced both monsters and miracles. Factories, Bingo, Mosques, Country Music, Leprosy, Theatre, Socialism and Lipton's Tea all somehow combine in one petri dish. The community bears the scars of a city constantly reinventing itself.

N

Jean Luc Nancy Nancy's work on community is summarised by *La Communauté désœuvrée* (*The Inoperative Community*, 1982). He argues that community has been the dominant issue in contemporary history, interpreting it as something that can be reduced on the one hand to a definition of society as an economic union or on the other hand as a mystical, blood community such as the fascist model.

Nancy prefers to define community as a resistance to the power a group can acquire when it reduces itself to a single thing. The multiple, diverse and contradictory elements of an open community preserve its health.

Nostalgia The Occident has rendered itself to the nostalgia for a more archaic community that has disappeared, and to deploring a loss of familiarity, fraternity and conviviality. Our history begins with the departure of Ulysses and with the onset of rivalry, dissension, and conspiracy in his palace. Around Penelope, who reweaves the fabric of intimacy without ever managing to complete it, pretenders set up the warring and political scene of society – pure exteriority.   Jean Luc Nancy, *The Inoperative Community*, 1982

O

Orang-utan Man – wonderful Man, with divine face, turned towards heaven, he is not a deity, his end under present form will come ... he is no exception. – he possesses some of the same general instincts and feelings as animals.

Let man visit Ourang-outang in domestication, hear its expressive whine, see its intelligence when spoken [to]; as if it understands every word said – see its affection. – to those it knew. – See its passion & rage, sulkiness, & very actions of despair ... [L]et him look at the savage, roasting his parent, naked, artless, not improving yet improvable & let him dare to boast of his pre-eminence.   Charles Darwin in Burkhardt, F., et al., *Darwin's Scientific Diaries 1836–1842*, 1987

P

Partners *They talk about the good old days. Some was good and others were maybe… Because when you were a woman you had an ordeal because the men did nothing. They went out and worked and they did nothing and on a Friday night they thought they had the right to take half of the money and go to the pub with it. You were left with the other half. To survive with everything. Clothes, feed families, pay the rent. Everything. The electricity bill.*

And they went…I mean they thought they had the god-given right to do that and I quite admire what's going on now because my daughters don't stand for that. The money's tabled you know what I mean – that's for the mortgage, that's for this, and that's for that.

Pawn *Years ago, when you didn't have much money, my husband's uncle died. So, he was going to the funeral so I thought I had nothing else but to get to the room and get his suit out and get a wee press up because in they days the suits crumpled dead easy. And where's his suit? So, when he comes in I says to him 'Yours suits not in the wardrobe'. He had the suit he was married in. He held on to it. I says, 'Where is it?'.*

'I don't know.'

'You must know where your suit is.'

So, back into the wardrobe again, looking on the ledges, and I find the pawn ticket. He had pawned his suit for a drink. So I had to go along and ask my mother to lend me 21 shillings to get this suit out the pawn. So I says, 'When I get it I will re-pawn it back again to give you the money.' And it cost you sixpence, a wee sixpence, to get it wrapped if you wanted. We couldn't afford to get it wrapped. So, walking back with

it on your arm.

Aye, but anyway, I got this suit and I brought it back and I says, 'I will give it a steam press for wearing for the funeral.' As I was steam pressing his suit (the gents always wore a white hankie here) I said 'Oh, that hankie needs changing, I will put a fresh hankie in.' I took it out and put a fresh one in and I went like that – 35 shillings fell out of this hankie. And he had pawned it for 21 shillings.

The money was his?

Aye. He had forgot about it. He had more in his pocket than he had pawned, aye.

Plain Slicer *Food wise it's changed terrible. That's why we always try to cook by the way… I cook all of mine. I make my own dinners when I am here. Aye, I make them soup and I make…*

That's what I do as well for mine and I buy, I get my wain organic stuff because I can tell you there is a difference.

Oh there is.

So Elizabeth, Elizabeth doesn't buy anything else, buys it for me now and again. She brings up organic this and that.

My Susan is the same but I don't buy it. I try though.

So, I used to so during the war when you couldn't get nothing. It was rationed and that my mother used to get a plain loaf, you don't see plain loaves nowadays.

The slicer.

A plain slicer. A cottage loaf, jam it and put another slice, half it and quarter it, wee quarters like that, and my mother made her own batter like you would do for fish. She never bought it, she made it. It was great. Didn't she, Sadie?

Oh aye.

And she made it and put it in this chip pan…

Chuck the bread in it.

Chuck the bread in it and put it in the chip pan and it come up like big fritters.

We waited on that coming out. It was glorious. Do you know there is, I was telling my daughters about this, I was reading in the paper there is some big restaurant up the town is got that as a delicacy, did you read that Sadie?

Pomegranates *The pomegranates we used to get.*

The size we used to get, big giant…

Never ate a lot of sweeties, we never did it.

The sweet shop, the sweet shop in Cumberland Street did you…? George and John and they had stairs going down to the cellar an they made beetroot down there.

Everything was fresh you know.

Went to get fresh beetroot and to the chemist for ascetic acid and that would get diluted. My auntie Mary always used to slice up the beetroot put some sugar in the jar and then put some ascetic acid in the jar and that was your jar of beetroot and she used to get umpteen jars out of a pound of beetroot.

When my father, when my father was here, he was an ice cream man, he had a cart and a bicycle and the ice cream was in it peddled everywhere and sold his ice cream. He was Velenti's the ice cream supplier then, Velenti's.

Velenti, aye.

And my father won a top prize for selling the most ice cream. My mother used to say, 'I think he gives it to all the dogs you know.' But then he made popcorn, and it was my mother who made the popcorn. She was really good and she made it in squares and she used grease proof paper and she would put it in and I always remember my father going out in the close and shouting 'Candy popcorn thruppence a go!' Candy popcorn, that was how he made his money, selling popcorn and ice cream and all that.

Don't forget the apples.

Premonitions Premonitions cover a spectrum from human intuition to a sense of the supernatural. At their most logical, premonitions of a future event are the product of subliminal mental processing. All known information is collated and

a likely result is predicted though as this happens at an unconscious level, it appears miraculous. Other predictions occur with no apparent information to hand, an intuitive leap so great that the supernatural is invoked in the absence of any clear explanation.

Architecture seems to inhabit a similar spectrum. As an art form that not only tries to foresee the future but attempts to shape it as well, it involves a degree of prediction that can determine the lives of a population.

Providence *See how the wee ones get something every week, when we get something Easter and Christmas…*

If you were lucky.

Pubs *Doyle's pub was famous – it's still there but it's not the same, it used to be a very ornamental place, full of Irish pubs – Doyle's Pub was famous – if there wasn't a fight you got your money back (laughing) … aye, it wis a wild place, you got black, and it was the same after mass, at St John's – all the Irish people always stood outside, that's where the news spread about – everybody, anybody that wis over, they always started 'guess who's dead – getaway, and then they would start on the living (laughing) – even when visitors used to come up to the house – have you noticed that yourself with Irish people? – do you know who's dead, right away before they start, aye, aye … any good news would come after, who's getting married, who's got a child and that, but aye … 'auld Finnegan's dead – Jesus, when did he die – last week – oh …*

Q

Quotidian This is the three R's
The three R's:
Repetition, Repetition, Repetition

Mark E. Smith, *Repetition*

R

Rent *The rent was one pound eight shillings, something like that, forty pence a week and we used to struggle getting it together, one pound and eight shillings and it was a struggle getting that together wasn't it?*

Renovation *Glasgow's a new city and its been rebuilt, its been rebuilt with a bit of thought and a lot of care to its history. You know because it is a busy area. My Mum was talking on Sunday to a friend of hers and he was saying where's Claire's flat and she was saying its in the Gorbals. The Gorbals, he said, Christ you wouldn't have lived in the Gorbals, you wouldn't have walked down the street in the Gorbals without a gun, he said, twenty years ago and now everybody wants to live there you know, so it has developed.*

S

Shops *I don't know if you know this street but you never had to go into the town.*
One end of the street to other every shop was there.
Every shop you need.
Even a first communion shop for the wee dresses for the kids making their first communion.
Aye, sold everything, and they had a system – a cup that took your money. It went right round the shop.
I remember that system. You just cupped it on and pulled it and it went away, took it right round the whole shop.
You had to wait for a pod to give you your change, it honestly it took…
It was brilliant. That street had about nine butchers, didn't it, easy. Nine butchers. You took your pick.
You see this. I don't think you can beat the personal touch. All the local grocers that we

*used to go to, but the personal touch, and you got a laugh, you know what I mean,
a chat and you can't beat that. Now you are going in and you are just self-service.*

*If you didn't turn up from one day to the next, somebody would knock your door to see
if you were sick. It was just buzzing with activity.*

It was great.

Spence, Basil Basil Spence, Scottish Architect (1907–1976). Spence's career is dominated by two commissions – Coventry Anglican Cathedral (1962) and the Queen Elizabeth Square flats in the Gorbals area of Glasgow (1965). Coventry Cathedral was built beside the ruins of the old cathedral, destroyed during the blanket bombing of the city in the Second World War.

The conception of the new cathedral is seldom considered in its larger cultural context. The late 40s and 50s in Britain were austere and grey but there was a sense of spirituality and optimism that often seemed founded on a new sense of British history (and the realm saved from the enemy). This ethos is clear in many of Powell and Pressburger's films of the time – *I Know Where I'm Going* or *The Canterbury Tales* for example. It's also evident in the compositions of Benjamin Britten and Michell Tippett, both of whom presented new work for the inauguration of Spence's Coventry Cathedral (Britten's *War Requiem* and Tippett's *King of Priam*). The Cathedral itself can be seen as a highpoint of the now forgotten post war cultural moment.

The Queen Elizabeth Square flats were born from the same optimism, a vision of the future that would wipe away the squalor of the slums. The flats, however, never achieved their aim. While early residents remained divided on their architectural value, the area including the flats quickly degenerated through lack of maintenance, high unemployment and the attendant problems of drugs and gangs. Their demolition in 1993 was welcomed by the city as a whole and may be seen as a very public attempt to begin the eradication of the 1960s Modernist legacy in the city.

Sweets *Just an ordinary chip pan with lard in it, no oil, aye. A regular pan, no timer, nothing on it.*

It is the jam is heated up and the batter is on the inside and it is all heated up, melts in your mouth. It is lovely.

These things you didn't buy, you made rice semolina and sago. Stewed apples.

On the whole the kids were better fed years ago because these jars… We never bought these jars.

Didn't have half the sweet stuff they have now.

Couldn't afford it.

That's how you get diabetes. That is true, I believe that.

My mother was having her last baby and we didn't have much. There was a fruit shop in the Gorbals and there was a Coyle's in Corn Street and she gave me a thruppenny bit to go up to Coyle's and get thruppence of chipped fruit. That was fruit that half of it was off, and they would chip the bad bit, and they would give you the good bit, and you would get a bag of chipped fruit. That was the notion she had when she was pregnant. And she never gave us any, I went for the fruit and she never gave us any.

Did she make stewed apples and that Susan?

No she just sat and ate it and you were glad of it. My Da used to eat chipped fruit and it was a luxury. I used to eat cooking apples. I couldn't eat the apples today but I used to sit and eat a cooking apple.

T

The Twelfth *And they used to, whit they used tae dae on the 12th – there wis Neptune Street and the called it 'The Irish Channel' – right – and they used to go down there wi their flute bands playing, and the windows used to open, there wur those big chamber pots, ye know, wi the two hands, filled tae the brim, bang – year after year they went*

doon that street, and they've taken some causalities! – and they didnae even take their causalities tae the Southern General – they went up tae the Royal.

Twomax[1] The Twomax Building was a reliable source of employment in the Gorbals throughout the nineteenth and twentieth centuries. When cotton production ceased there in the 1860s, it was used for other purposes – most recently for clothing manufacturing.

The building dates from 1821 and it is the oldest surviving iron-framed cotton mill in Glasgow. The iron frame was meant to render the structure fireproof and that method of construction became a commonplace throughout the city.

Twomax[2] *Your sister worked in the Twomax factory.*

Oh yeah she was there.

Jumpers, they made, woollen suits like skirts and jumpers. Mainly ladies stuff, you know. Supplied really big top class shops in the world. A good knitwear factory it was. The clothes used to go to Lewis' and Frasers. They were very exclusive, aye. And yet, see the ladies suits – the jackets and skirts, I am talking outdoor. You know, they were really very expensive, you could see the money's worth there. That's what was made in Twomax.

They washed up, didn't they?

Aye.

And are all the older people gone?

Maggie Cole was the last one I remember. She retired. It turned into something else, just go and pick stuff but it was never the same 'cause I think I bought a coat actually and I don't think it was Twomax …

She worked in it when she was only a lassie…

So she did aye.

She worked in it until she got married but Maggie Moores worked until she retired you know. Remember the hair works.

What's hair works?

Mattresses.
They called it a hair works but it was hair stuffed in and they built the mattresses in it.
You had a comfortable bed in a hair mattress didn't you?

U

Upside Down Ye poor take courage,
ye rich take care
This earth was made a common treasury
for everyone to share
All things in common,
all people one
Leon Rosselon, *World Turned Upside Down*

V

St Valentine The bones of St Valentine are said to reside in the church of Blessed John Duns Scotus in the Gorbals – donated to the friars by a French family. That fact is disputed by Irish Carmelites who claim the saint's remains lie at Whitefriar Street Church in Dublin. Whatever the truth of the matter it is an enduring irony that the saint most associated with romantic love is said to dwell in the area of Glasgow most associated with violence throughout history.
Oddly, the greatest meditation on love and sex in the Gorbals may be Alexander Trocchi's erotic novel, *Thongs*. The book tells the story of a young woman living in the area whose father is a notorious 'razor king'. Growing up with violence, the girl becomes aware of her own leanings towards masochism and, after a process of self discovery, she ends up voluntarily crucified on a hillside in Spain.

W

Wemyss pigs 'Wemyss Ware' was first produced in Fife in 1882 and named after the family in Wemyss Castle who were early collectors of the pottery's work. Robert Heron ran the enterprise and employed continental painters he had encountered on his European grand tour. A Bohemian, Karel Nekola, became the best known of these artists and his style came to epitomise Wemyss Ware.

The pottery was forced to close in the 1930s during the depression though the brand was bought for use in Devon and later became part of Royal Doulton.

The Wemyss pig was the pottery's most famous product, closely followed by their cat figurines. The pigs that are most prized have been decorated with green shamrocks or clover and they have become rare collector's items, fetching prices in the tens of thousands. The pigs were often made as decoration for nurseries or bedrooms, occasionally as paper weights or piggy banks and sometimes as bottles to carry whisky on New Year 'first footing' expeditions.

Work *This place was buzzing with work places, there were work places everywhere, wasn't there Sue?*

Aye, you were never without a job.

Wains could come out of school and start a job the next day.

X

Xenotransplants The child's chest was opened and her heart removed. The implantation of the animal heart took about one hour, after which the child's blood temperature was returned to normal, her new heart started and her body weaned slowly from the heart-lung machine, according to the hospital.

Hospital spokesmen said the operation profited from experience in the transplant of ape organs, including kidney xenotransplants performed in the early 1960s and the use of baboons in humans with liver failure. Jay Mathews and Howard Kurtz, *Baboon-Heart Baby Improves*, The Washington Post, October 28, 1984

Y

Yeast Yeasts are single-celled (unicellular) fungi, a few species of which are commonly used to leaven bread, or ferment alcoholic beverages.

Yeast fermentations comprise the oldest and largest application of microbial technology. Baker's yeast is used for bread production, brewer's yeast is used for beer fermentation, and yeast is also used for wine fermentation. More recently, yeast has been used to drive experimental fuel cells and a report in Wired claims that:

> At the University of California at Berkeley, mechanical engineering professor Liwei Lin is busy developing a microbial fuel cell that runs off the digestive activity of baker's yeast. The yeast feed on glucose, a simple sugar, and digest it in a process called aerobic metabolism.
>
> "We extract electrons from the yeast cells where the aerobic metabolism process happens", Lin explains.
>
> Controlling the movement of electrons to harness a renewable source of fuel remains the target for scientists designing fuel cells, which extract power from electrochemical reactions. The advantage of Lin's mechanism is that it runs on glucose, a naturally abundant resource produced by plants.
>
> One of his small prototypes, measuring 0.7 square centimetres and less than 1 millimetre thick, produces 1 microwatt of power – approximately enough to power a digital wristwatch.
>
> Lin believes it is only a matter of time before fuel cells in laptop

computers will recharge from glucose cartridges. He plans to adapt his prototype to use glucose found in the bloodstream to power implantable devices such as internal pacemakers.

Z

Ziggurat The earliest examples of ziggurats date from the end of the third millennium BC and the latest date from the sixth century BC. Built in receding tiers upon a rectangular, oval, or square platform, the ziggurat was a pyramidal structure. Sun-baked bricks made up the core of the ziggurat with facings of fired bricks on the outside.

The facings were often glazed in different colours and may have had cosmological significance. The number of tiers ranged from two to seven, with a shrine or temple at the summit. Access to the shrine was provided by a series of ramps on one side of the ziggurat or by a spiral ramp from base to summit. Notable examples of this structure include the ruins at Ur and Khorsabad in Mesopotamia. [Spirals reference the movement of consciousness or the Golden Ratio.]

The Mesopotamian ziggurats were not the place of public worship or ceremonies but instead were believed to be dwelling places for the gods. Through the ziggurat the gods could be close to mankind and each city had its own patron god or goddess. It has also been suggested that the ziggurat was a symbolic representation of the primeval mound upon which the universe had supposedly been created.

Moreover, the ziggurat may have been built as a bridge between heaven and Earth.

The Tower of Babel may have been the ziggurat at Marduk in Babylon and its name evokes one the greatest stories of architectural hubris:

And as men migrated from the east, they found a plain in the land of

Corpus

S^{ti} Valentini,

Martyris.

*The Body of
St Valentine,
Martyr.*

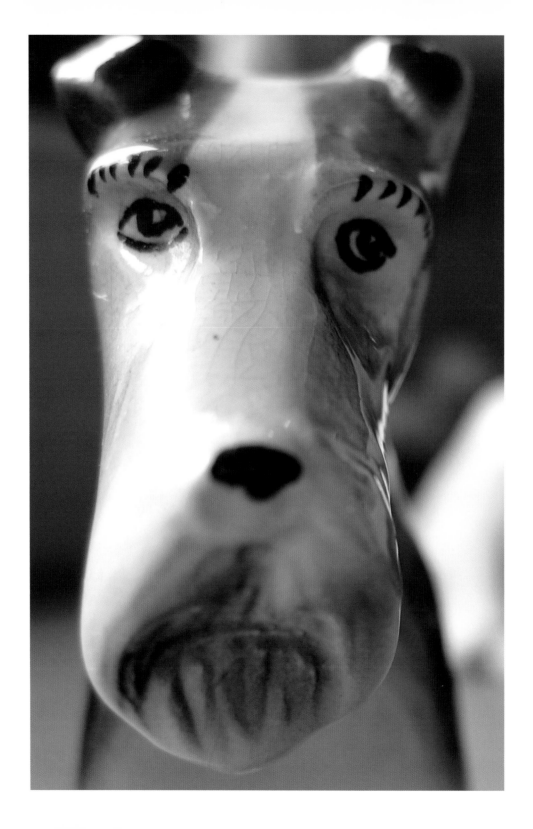

Shinar and settled there. And they said to one another, "Come, let us make bricks, and burn them thoroughly." And they had brick for stone, and bitumen for mortar. Then they said, "Come, let us build ourselves a city, and a tower with its top in the heavens, and let us make a name for ourselves, lest we be scattered abroad upon the face of the whole earth." And the LORD came down to see the city and the tower, which the sons of men had built. And the LORD said, "Behold, they are one people, and they have all one language; and this is only the beginning of what they will do; and nothing that they propose to do will now be impossible for them. Come, let us go down, and there confuse their language, that they may not understand one another's speech." So the LORD scattered them abroad from there over the face of all the earth, and they left off building the city. Genesis, 11: 2–8

SS/mf

23rd February 2005

HOMES

PARAGON: REQUESTED FEEDBACK ON THE INDIVIDUAL ARTWORK

Daphne Wright, the Artist commissioned to create the particular piece of artwork received by you at settlement is in the process of researching material for the book that she is writing. The book will include the themes behind each artwork and the research gathered prior to and during fabrication, an essay by a leading curator and cultural theorist along with various interviews including the architect Piers Gough, homeowners, the development company and other members of the Gorbals community.

Daphne Wright has requested that we write to you to undertake an informal 'one to one' interview with her to obtain your feedback on the artwork you received. The interview would take place in your home and be conducted as an audio recording but photography of yourself with your artwork may be requested. We hope that some of the interviews will be included in the finished publication of the book any participants will also be invited to attend the private launch scheduled for the Autumn.

Daphne Wright is planning to come to Glasgow on 15th & 16th March 2005 to underake the interviews and collect the final material for the book, therefore if you would like to participate in this opportunity, please contact Rhona Warwick at The Artworks Programme by phone or email to arrange a suitable time for an interview. Contact details are as undernoted:

The Artworks Programme
34 Stanley Street
Glasgow
G41 1JB

T: 0141 418 0439
F: 0141 429 0861

Email: info@theartworksprogramme.org http://www.theartworksprogramme.org/

Thank you for your assistance.

Yours sincerely

Sarah Stanger
Sales & Marketing Director

Home Ornaments

Simon Morrissey

Picture this group of objects. They are domestic in scale, things you can easily imagine people having on their shelves at home. As a group they are certainly peculiar. Variations in scale create a diorama from an unmade B-movie about the day humanity shrank. A long, low, bleached model of a Modernist tower-block is surrounded by grossly enlarged elements from the natural world. Huge soft grey woollen cacti fringe the settlement. A massive photograph of a benign ape in an ornate frame stands at its opposite edge, like a giant billboard of the face of an animal dictator that is supposed to reinforce a myth of benevolence in the minds of its subjects. A fat blue ceramic rodent dwarfs the building with its sheer bulk as it eats from a feeding bowl, whilst a gaudy embroidered parrot with a disturbingly decorated face looks on from its perch. The motley collection of animals ignore each other in their self-absorption and all in turn ignore the fact that the tower-block is collapsing under the mushrooming effects of an explosion at its far end. The people, unsurprisingly, are nowhere to be seen.

No matter how idiosyncratic the result, the desire to project associations onto objects, and then build narratives from these associations, is a common tendency. These narratives vary depending on our relationship to the objects – and some things prompt this reaction more than others – but they are projected onto them nevertheless because once something is put out into the world it cannot exist in a vacuum, even if sometimes some things wish to.

Art can be one of those things, and those that make it can sometimes appear allergic to the very suggestion that art might generate such narrative association – despite their lack of ability to prevent it being attached to what they make. Perhaps this is because the narratives that can be projected onto art often have little to do with what the work actually is and everything to do with what people want it to do for them. From objects to knowledge, nothing can escape its placement within complex territories of use and ownership.

Daphne Wright's *Home Ornaments* acknowledges these inevitabilities, exploits the extrapolation of narrative and deliberately agitates the idea of ownership in an attempt to remain slippery within this double grasp. *Home Ornaments* is the collective name for the group of objects described above. As their title suggests, the objects are a series of ornaments designed to be kept in people's homes. And it is not only the relationship between these objects, highlighted by the somewhat absurd narrative that can be drawn from the objects when they are placed together, that is peculiar about the work. Its status is also peculiar, and doubly so when one is aware that it was created within the context of public art. Public art is not only particularly vulnerable to the contentions over meaning and ownership that can surround art, but it is also a context in which these contentions create expectations of how art should be made and behave that can be particularly narrowly conceived.

Despite contemporary art's diverse manifestations and positions, public art often finds it difficult to escape being constrained by the agendas behind its commissioning. Almost exclusively, public art's status is as an aid to programmes of economic and social regeneration or is funded as a generator of social focus and identity. The very fact that public art more often than not has to be justified in these terms by those commissioning it sets up a web of expectations, obligations and orthodoxies that limit its potential. Some of these orthodoxies may appear old, such as public art's contin-uing tendency to manifest itself as permanently sited sculptural work outdoors. Others appear more recent, and in fact may not even be generally thought of as orthodoxies as yet. One of these new tendencies is a preoccupation with drawing on the social and cultural contexts in which the art will be sited as a generator of the

substance of the work. Although this approach to making art has in part revitalised a once moribund area, it is in danger of becoming a new orthodoxy with an equally constraining effect on the conception of public art. It could in fact become more insidious than the old fashioned preoccupation with plonking sculpture outdoors in that it allows public art to portray a new diversity in terms of its form, but engenders a sense of obligation that threatens to make public art even more illustrative of external agendas.

The context in which Wright produced *Home Ornaments* displays many of these defining characteristics of public art's complex constraints. The work was commissioned by The Artworks Programme on behalf of the Crown Street Regeneration Project – the third wholesale redevelopment of the Gorbals, Glasgow, to take place in 150 years. The Gorbals is perhaps Glasgow's most infamous district, with a rich history to match its notoriety. Synonymous with poverty, overcrowding and the rise of gang culture, the Gorbals was, however, also a powerhouse of the Industrial Revolution and became a culturally diverse haven for immigrants from all over Europe. Major influxes of Jewish immigration from Eastern Europe in the late nineteenth century were added to by equally significant immigration from Ireland in the early twentieth century. Overcrowding led to the deterioration of the housing stock and by the mid-1950's the cycle of immigration had turned with vast numbers of Gorbals residents migrating to new towns. The Modernist dreams of the 1960's redevelopment failed to bear fruit, and so in 1990 the Crown Street Regeneration Project was initiated to replace it with a mixture of speculative private housing & social accommodation for rent.

Wright was commissioned specifically to mark the rebuilding of Queen Elizabeth Square, where deteriorating social housing designed by the architect Sir Basil Spence was replaced with a complex of 127 privately-owned apartments designed by CZWG Architects for the developer Cruden Group. Given Wright's previous work, which was predominantly sculptural and was increasingly manifesting itself on a large scale, it would have been logical to expect her to make a publicly-sited sculpture, as many of the other artists in the programme had. *Home Ornaments* could indeed be seen as sculpture of a sort in that it is comprised of fabricated objects, but in every other sense it is the antithesis of all we expect from public sculpture.

Although her brief was essentially open, The Artworks Programme commissioned Wright and the other artists involved in the redevelopment to "work with new and existing communities to explore the fundamental questions about the character of the place during this period of transition."[1] Wright was equally wary of the idea of working too closely with the community in the process of creating her work as she was of imposing a piece of work on the urban landscape and a disinterested audience. During her initial engagement with the commission, Wright participated in a number of processes that were designed to allow the community to feel a sense of connection to the commissioning process. When The Artworks Programme presented the ideas for commissions to the public on the streets of the Gorbals, Wright witnessed other artists in the programme face vociferously negative comment from members of the community. It was her first real experience of the contention over ownership and meaning of the commissioned artwork being played out. The idea that the members of the community were prepared to be exceptionally vocal about what they wanted the art to be and do fascinated Wright. She asked these outspoken, often older, members of the public what they wanted the artworks to represent and was met with a desire for statues of soldiers and mill workers – public monuments that valourised the common man.

This very traditional idea of public art impressed itself upon the artist precisely because it was so far from what even the most conventional contemporary art commissioner was likely to facilitate. This mis-match prompted Wright to start thinking about the idea of her work directly engaging with these conflicting desires, of making a piece of work that somehow avoided stereotypical modes of operation and critically questioned the expectations projected onto public art by all its different constituents – commissioner, funder, art-world, community.

Wright threw herself into a series of in-depth interviews with a broad section of the Gorbals public, in order to create a picture of the history of the social and cultural complexities of the area. Through this trawl of individual opinion and memory, anecdote and nostalgia, Wright learnt about the immigrant communities, the dominant industries of the area, the role of religion in the area, hardship and any number of other well rehearsed entries in the Gorbals communal consciousness. It would be easy and undoubtedly politically advantageous to claim that *Home Ornaments* arose directly out of these collaged fragments of narrative. But Daphne Wright's working processes are the direct opposite of this kind of literal translation. And although the work does draw on the histories and opinion Wright collected from the community, to describe this as a direct relationship would misrepresent the idiosyncratic and often opaque associative processes involved in the creation of her work.

For example, the idea that it was Wright's exploration of the histories of the area's local industries that prompted her decision to commission a series of small objects manufactured by craft producers provides a motivation for Wright's decision that is easily appreciated by all. The nature of these industries did tangentially influence the material form of some of the objects. However, the decision to make ornaments to be displayed in people's homes was in fact directly motivated by Wright's temporary job in the china and glass department of her local John Lewis department store in Bristol over the first Christmas during her project.

As an artist who draws on whimsical or sentimental fragments from popular and folk culture to explore universal concerns, Wright became fascinated with the decorative objects people would buy for themselves and as gifts. She was equally fascinated by the ideas of value that circulated around ornaments as she was by the objects themselves: the prices people would pay for them; what was seen as beautiful and what was not; people's investment in collecting them; and their appreciation of the sophisticated craft that was often involved in the ornaments' manufacture. This began a chain of thought about the status of art in the public consciousness that linked directly with Wright's desire to somehow critically question the expectations of public art. Ornaments are popular art rather than contemporary art and thus it would be easy to assume they are more democratic in their appeal. The fundamental contradiction, however, is that although seemingly democratic, ornaments are as contentious in their status as art. One person's beautiful cat made of shells is another person's ugly tat, while that person's prized collection of egg cups with comedy feet is simply unfathomable in the eyes of someone whose shelves sport realistic models of dogs, and so on. Ornaments are as susceptible to contention over aesthetics, meaning and value as works of art, and perhaps more susceptible to the projection of narrative and the associated – and often disproportionate – investment of emotion.

The idea of the ornament therefore offered Wright a vehicle through which she could directly explore the contention of value and meaning on an apparently democratic level. Paradoxically ornaments also presented her with something that would directly challenge democratic opinion. This is based on the simple fact that although people may own and appreciate ornaments within their own homes they do not think of them as art. Their expectations of ornaments are fundamentally separate from their expectations of art, and of public art in particular. In publicly framing her work as ornaments to be placed in people's homes Wright not only deliberately prompted the only too-common contention that her work simply 'wasn't art' at all, but also specifically contradicted the popular understanding of public art. Rather than her work being sited in some easily accessible communal space and therefore being commonly understood as public, Wright replaced this arena with the individual home – a space that is practically, and popularly understood to be, private.

In doing so, Wright placed *Home Ornaments* on fundamentally unstable ground where it would not be easily categorised as ordinary ornament, as art, or as public art

in the eyes of the people who would become the direct audience for the work. As fundamental as this expected popular reaction was in motivating Wright's thinking, an equally important motivation was the work's potential to disrupt the expectations of those familiar with contemporary art's varying strategies. Throughout her career Daphne Wright has produced work that manipulates and misdirects art-world orthodoxies. Her work has drawn on traditional materials and equally traditional ideas of sculpture, such as the representational cast, in a simulation of conventional strategies and concerns. Even when not deploying these strategies Wright's work is laboriously crafted. This prompts some viewers and critics to misread Wright's work as being conventional in its aspirations also – more interested in the display of technical virtuosity than in the communication of ideas. However, Wright has combined these strategies with disjointed soundtracks and obscure references to create deliberate deceptions and mis-readings that afford her work a particular autonomy from literal interpretation and confound such easy categorisations.

Wright continued this exploitation of craft skill as a mask behind which critical ideas are hidden in *Home Ornaments*. And it is important to stress that in terms of their generation the objects are indeed ornaments created as any other ornament might be, not pre-existing ornaments that have been elevated from popular culture and awarded the status of art through the artist's appropriation. In fact *Home Ornaments* are the reversal of this now commonplace Duchampian device. They are art in which the object is downgraded to the status of the decorative, a perversely self-deprecating gesture that is more critical of art's own unthinking orthodoxies than it is of any allegiance to skill, representational accuracy and attractiveness that may characterise popular aesthetics.

Wright decided that rather than making any of the ornaments herself, all the objects would be crafted by professional makers within the chosen genre of each ornament. She employed model-makers, ceramicists, embroiderers, religious statue painters,

and knitting designers to realise her ideas, as well as specialist companies to complete elements of the fabrication. Through doing so she produced a series of five objects that conform to the codes of manufacture that only skilled craftsmen in a particular field can produce. Wright's ornaments therefore behave as genuine ornaments. For example the model of Basil Spence's tower-block, *The Architect's Plan*, is made from the same cast polyurethane resin that fake-ivory tourist souvenirs are made from and *Pet Guinea Pig* is made of dyed slip-cast porcelain. They are all highly decorative and exceptionally highly crafted. They are almost embarrassing as contemporary sculpture. But this awkward position has been carefully sought after. What Wright has achieved in the deliberate positioning of the work so that it can be misread as reductive or nostalgic or traditional is an agitation of assumptions about how the work has been made, how it is positioned and what ideas it represents.

The peculiarity of each object and the group as a whole slowly introduces doubts that un-pick any easy assumption projected on to *Home Ornaments*. Perhaps the easiest ornament to locate is the scale model of the Basil Spence tower-block. The model captures the iconic block at the start of the process of demolition, as the first explosion ripped through the end of the building. Based on a photograph of the event, the model is a crappy souvenir of the moment the Modernist dream finally admitted defeat, and thus represents a complex emotional mixture of hope, failure and resentment.

If Spence's collapsing Modernist icon is the historical anchor for *Home Ornaments*, *Cacti Collection* is its future trajectory. The piece was inspired by collapsing disparate references together: an eccentric book on three dimensional knitting found in a charity shop, the history of textile production in the area, a reoccurring fascination with cacti as metaphors, and the ready-made discount Modern lifestyle of Ikea. The tone of *Cacti Collection* is hard to locate, however. Is it an acerbic comment on the aesthetics of the interiors of the new flats or a celebration of handicraft traditions? We are given few clues with which to un-pick its meaning.

Three out of five of the ornaments take the form of animals in one way or the other, a bias that reflects the sheer volume of animal ornaments Wright encountered on her trawls through second hand shops, craft books and department stores. *Pet Guinea Pig* could be seen as a reflection of local children's deep identification with keeping the animal, a re-imagining of the famously Scottish Wymess pig ornaments, or as a parody of the sophisticated objects made by companies such as Wedgwood that Wright spent endless hours selling in John Lewis. None of these influences convey the objects strangely confrontational presence, however, which is much more attributable to coincidences within its manufacture. The work was cast from a taxidermy guinea pig Wright purchased from a shop. Not being overly familiar with the animal Wright had not realised that the guinea pig had been incorrectly stuffed so that it was standing up on fully extended legs. This characteristic has lead to the object receiving the dubious accolade of being dubbed 'The Gorbals' Rat' by locals.

Fidelma, the gaudy embroidered parrot, and *Uncle*, a picture of an orang-utan in a hand-made gesso frame, are both even more entangled presences. Both draw on Wright's interest in ideas of sentimentality, in the tendency to bestow anthropomorphic qualities on animals, and the narratives of self-determination that are circulated and mutate within immigrant communities. These mix with abiding fascinations with objects such as the death-mask of a dead ape, religious icons and home-made toys to create something akin to animal familiars to be imposed on the area's mythology – the parrot as oracle and the orang-utan as clan elder.

The insertion of *Home Ornaments* into their carefully chosen context was as much a part of the work as the objects themselves. One ornament was placed within each of the new flats. Wright produced a manual to accompany the ornaments, much like the manuals accompanying the white goods in the fitted kitchen of the flat. She also schooled the employees of the Cruden Group marketing suite in the thinking behind the project and how the new owners were to treat their ornament. The new owners

were told that they were free to look after it, hide it in the cupboard or swap it with someone else in the apartment block. Inevitably narratives, from the factual to the apocryphal, were attached to the pieces by the Cruden employees and passed on to the new owners. These included the story of Helen Tinney, the woman killed as a result of falling debris in the demolition of Hutcheson Court; that the mid-twentieth century fad for keeping exotic birds meant that when the old flats were knocked down lots of parrots were released to fly around the Gorbals wild; and that *Uncle* was supposed to be a portrait of a distant family member.

Wright has described this process of the staff embedding the ornaments in local narrative as 'indoctrinating' the new owners into the idea that the objects had a value beyond their physical appearance. But despite this attempt to thoroughly ground the work in a local context *Home Ornaments* still met with a mixed reaction. Reactions to the ornaments varied wildly, based on everything from aesthetic preference to ideas of monetary value to deep offence. Most owners who received 'The Gorbals' Rat' were unhappy with it, stating that *Pet Guinea Pig* was the least respectable object. The anecdote that *Uncle* was supposed to be a portrait of a distant family member – something that had been a joke at the artist's own expense – led to the work being seen as derogatory to Glaswegians. Some owners thought their work was 'a con' whilst others were fascinated by the stories they had been told about the objects or by the idea that they may have been given something that would accrue in financial value because it was art. Some owners are known to have hidden their ornament in a drawer, others to have thrown them away, whilst others are known to have rescued these discarded pieces in an attempt to build a complete collection.

The manual that accompanied the ornaments was deliberately opaque about their ownership. The introductory text intimated that the ornament belonged to the flat and should be passed on when the flat changed hands, but did not explicitly challenge the assumption that the ornament was private property. The ornaments were thus

HOME ORNAMENTS

MANUAL / USER GUIDE

PLEASE RETAIN THIS USER GUIDE FOR FUTURE REFERENCE

---

1. There are 127 apartments in the 'Paragon' designed by CZWG Architects for Cruden Group. There is a 'Home Ornament' for each individual apartment.

2. Each 'Home Ornament' is part of a limited edition specially made for the 'Paragon.'

3. A 'Home Ornament' has been placed in each apartment. The 'Home Ornament' is not fixed down and can be moved around if wished.

4. If a different work is preferred, the 'Home Ornament' can be swapped between the apartment owners. This may be a permanent or temporary arrangement, to be negotiated between owners. Example:- swapping collection cards.

5. If the owner dislikes the object in their apartment they can take it off show at any time and store it.

6. It is preferred that a 'Home Ornament' remains as part of the apartment and be placed back in its original position when and if the apartment changes hands.

USER INSTRUCTIONS

generally understood to be the private property of the new flat owners – who were predominantly incomers to the Gorbals – but were also understood to have been inspired by local stories and made for the wider community. This created tensions around the idea of who exactly constituted 'the community' and who precisely 'owned' the work. It is a portrait of exactly the contested ground Wright had hoped the project would engender: an agitated and genuine debate over the meaning and ownership of public art.

With *Home Ornaments* Wright has created a work that re-frames the parameters of public art in decisive ways. Both in its inspiration and its dissemination, the project conceives of the public arena as knowledge and narrative – and the way in which this circulates amongst us – rather than as any form of physical space. The project's conceptual structure is an expression of the fact that this public arena is accessed, filtered, moulded and interpreted in highly idiosyncratic ways by individuals. Mirroring this, the work lives multiple lives. Simultaneously tacky and exquisite, Wright's ornaments are physically a small set of obtuse presences but behind their deceptively decorative mask lies a direct critical reflection on the expectations around and orthodoxies within the creation and dissemination of public art. Both a repository for and generator of local narrative, *Home Ornaments* thrives on misinterpretation, the supposed opposition between public and private and the strong division of opinion. In doing so it functions as much through a secondary life of anecdote, argument and individual interpretation as it does as a series of objects, reinserting itself back into the public arena in the same way it came to exist.

1   www.theartworksprogramme.org

List of images

Daphne Wright
Home Ornaments

The Artworks Programme commissioned Home Ornaments for the Crown Street Regeneration Project, Gorbals, Glasgow, Scotland

The Artworks Programme
1149 – 1151 Cathcart Road
Glasgow G42 9HB, Scotland, UK
T: 0141 632 6735
E: info@theartworksprogramme.org
www.theartworksprogramme.org

Rhona Warwick installed the artworks into all the houses of the Paragon Development.

Home Ornaments was made by Janet Haigh, Tim Wright, Jane Wheeler, John Brennan, Hanne Rysgaard, Patrick Haines, Mark Plenderleith, Lisa Scantlebury and Phil Bowden.

The Home Ornaments manual was designed by Claire Carey.

This bookwork is an integral part of Daphne Wright's public art commission for the Gorbals. Funded from a "Percent for Art Scheme" of private contributions from seven housing developers appointed by the Crown Street Regeneration Project for Queen Elizabeth Square, Gorbals: Cruden Group, Miller Homes, Dawn Homes, Stewart Milne Homes, Ogilvie Homes and Tay Homes Scotland (now Redrow Homes Scotland). The artwork strategy initiated and managed by The Artworks Programme is also part funded by Scottish Enterprise Glasgow.

Daphne Wright is represented by Frith Street Gallery, London.

Frith Street Gallery
59–60 Frith Street
London W1D 3JJ
T: 0207 494 1550
E: info@frithstreetgallery.com
www.frithstreetgallery.com

The artist would like to thank:

All the people from the Gorbals who were interviewed as part of the project: Margaret Morgan, Mary Mc Taggart, Moira Rodgers, Sadie Peden, Margaret Flanagan, Susan Brolly, Bill Hay, Bill Steven, Lorna Wallace, Bill Sharkey and Willie McLean.

The home owners in Paragon Development: Chris Kelly, Moneeb Ahmed, Stephen Burk, Alan Blair and Gordon Lindsay, Claire Smyth, Mr. Smith and Ellen Osborough, Margaret McCrory, John Woods, Brian McGowan, Miss Aitchison, Gillian Crawford, Jane McDermot and Kirk O'Rourke.

The transcribers Kate Gaughan and Karen McGlone, and writer Laura Mansfield.

Piers Gough and David Donachie of CZWG Architects Ltd.

Liz Peden, Claire Flanagan and Noleen Begley from Gorbals Arts Project.

The children and staff from St Francis Primary School, Gorbals, Glasgow.

John Gallagher, Managing Director, Cruden Estates Ltd.; Allan Callaghan, Managing Director, Cruden Building and Renewals Ltd.; Dan Donald, Director, Cruden Estates Ltd.; Sarah Stanger, Sales Director, Cruden Homes Ltd.; Janice Belshaw and the Cruden Homes Ltd. Sales Team; Jacquie Sweeney, Secretary; Gerry Smith, Site Manager; Alan Burton, David McLatachie, Raymond McCafferty, Brian Hanson, Clare Battles, John Coleman, Evan Kilpatrick, Dominic Meina, Jim Smith, Yvander McLeod, Tam Bateman, Pat MacAdam and Steven Frame of the 'Paragon' construction team.

Matt Baker, Juliet Sebley and Rhona Warwick of The Artworks Programme.

Ben Harman, Gallery of Modern Art, Glasgow City Council.

Daphne Wright
Home Ornaments

Published by The Artworks Programme

Edited by Simon Morrissey
Designed by Herman Lelie and Stefania Bonelli
Printed by Graphicom, Italy
All photography © the artist except front cover, p. 83 © Jamie Woodley and
p. 54 © Bay View Books Ltd 1987
Texts © Francis McKee & Simon Morrissey

ISBN: 0-9514953-5-6

The artist would like to thank Simon, Francis, Herman, Stefania, Juliet, Rhona and John.

theartworksprogramme